GRIEF IS AN ORIGAMI SWAN

For the departed but not forgotten.

And for dad.

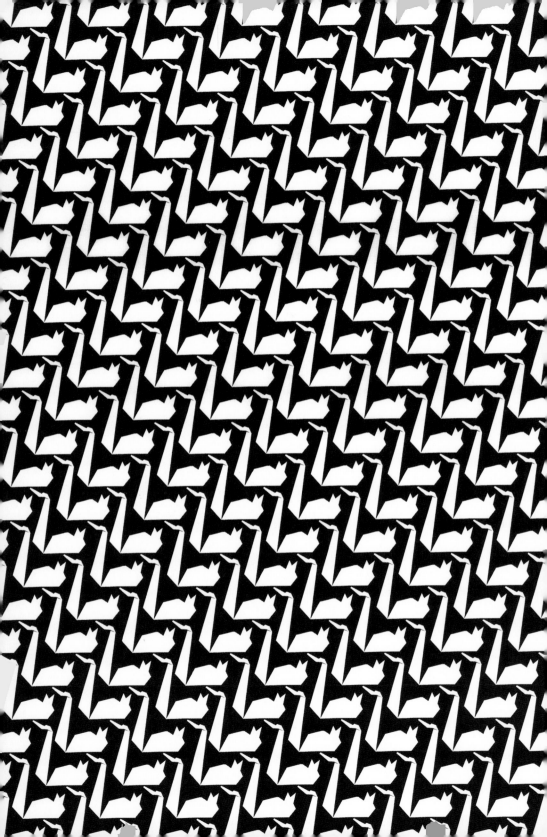

AN ART BOOK ABOUT GRIEF

grief is an origami swan

Michèle Saint-Michel

Published by Michelle Sander Media. MICHELLE SANDER
MEDIA and associated logos are trademarks and/or registered
trademarks of Michelle Sander and Michelle Sander Media.

The publisher does not have any control over and does not assume
any responsibility for author or third-party websites or their content.
Cover photo by David Cohen. Pressed organics with Sparrow &
Snow.

LIBRARY OF CONGRESS CATALOGING-IN-PUBLICATION DATA
Saint-Michel, Michèle.
Grief is an Origami Swan / by Michèle Saint-Michel. – 1st ed.
p.   cm.
ISBN: 978-0-9999020-1-1

Summary: Begin to process grief and remember those lost using the
art form of origami. Learn to fold an origami swan using origami
paper, and befriend the often confusing and sometimes unsettling
feelings experienced during bereavement and after loss. Grief has no
timeline and carries no expiration. Your feelings, as confusing as they
may be, are a valid and necessary part of the healing journey.

Paperback edition. Summer 2020.

In the midst of winter,
I found there was,
within me,
an invincible summer.

Albert Camus

Origami is the Japanese art of folding paper into decorative shapes and figures.

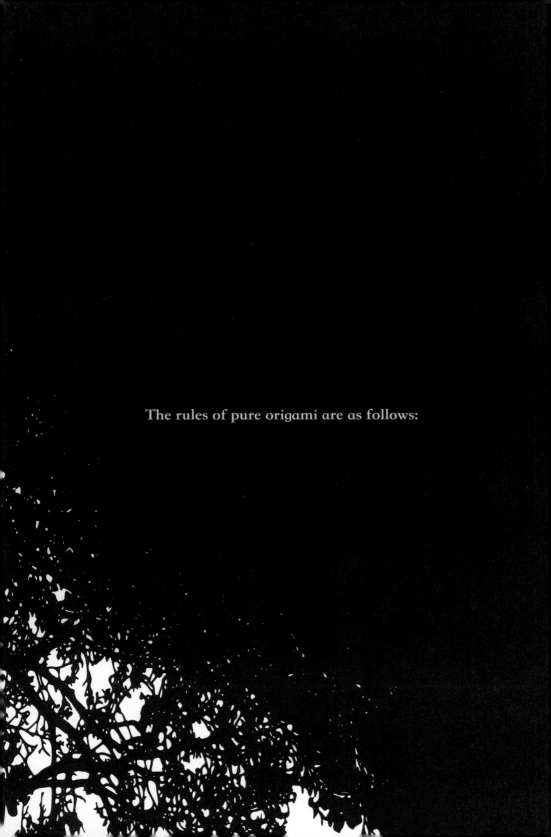

The rules of pure origami are as follows:

1. You must use a square sheet of paper.

2. You may not use scissors, glue, or tape.

3. You shall not decorate your figure after folding.

Grief, however, has no rules.

Grief has no timeline.

Grief is unknowable.
And it doesn't make any sense.

Grief comes and goes as it pleases.

And it will fill hours and sometimes weeks
long-stretching moments
and short years.

Grief is the suffering that fills the place
someone you love once filled.

And the missing

And the missi g

And the miss ng

And the mis in

And the mi si

And the m ssing

And the m ssing

And the missing will hurt

And it won't make any sense.

And you will forget things.
And you'll worry you
might forget everything,
everything about **them**,
but you won't.

And the missing

And the missing

And the missing

And the missing

And the missing

And the missing

And the missing

And the missing will hurt

And it won't make any sense.

And you will feel **heavy**
weighed down
and helpless.

And for many days you will do
nothing but sleep.

But some days you will do things.
And one day you will fold your first origami swan.

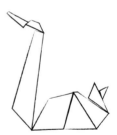

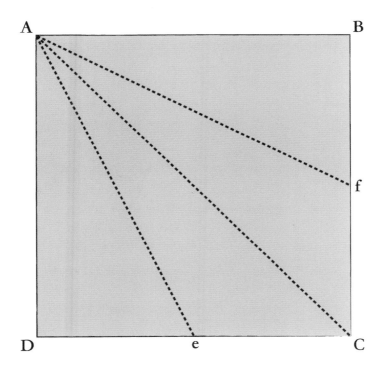

1. Place paper color-side down.

2. Valley fold A-C (like a taco), then unfold.

3. Valley fold A-e, bringing D to touch A-C crease.

4. Valley fold A-f, bringing B to touch A-C crease.

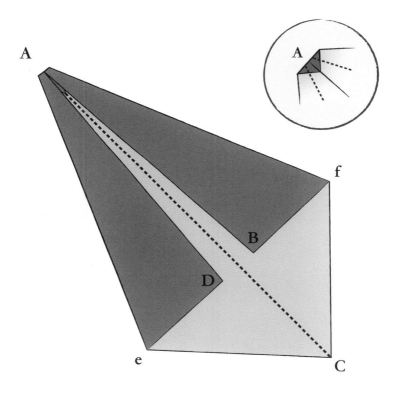

5. Unfold paper and make a small fold with A.

6. Refold flaps D and B over folded tip A.

7. Valley fold A-C (like a taco), bringing e to meet f.

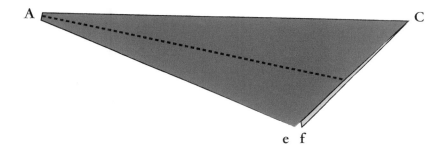

8. Along dashed line, fold A-e back up to meet the A-C crease.

9. Turn figure over and fold A-f to the A-C crease.

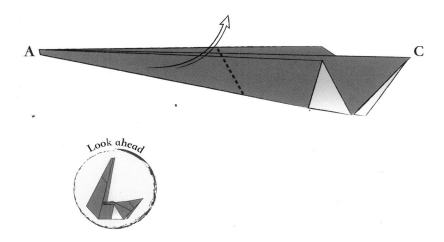

A

C

Look ahead

10. Outside reverse fold across dashed line.

Note: This fold can be tricky when first starting
out. After folding along dashed line, turn both
sides back to form the neck, as shown in the
Look ahead breakaway.
The swan should be able to sit upright on its own.

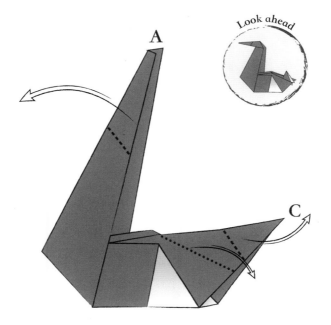

11. Inside reverse fold C down along dotted line.

12. Valley fold C up along dashed line, so the tail is pointing up.

13. Outside reverse fold A to form the head.

Look ahead

14. Similar to the tail, fold in and out along dotted line and dashed line to form the beak.

15. The folded origami swan in its final form. Majestic.

Remember: Origami is an art form. Respect your process. You will grow more comfortable with time and practice.

Tip: Using thin origami paper will make the task easier.

And there will be days when you miss them
because it's their birthday
or it's your birthday
or it's Flag Day
or it's a Wednesday.

And it won't make any sense, so
you'll fold an origami swan.

And there will be dreams where they feature. Right there next to you or talking to you and it will feel real, and you'll wake in anger and desperation, wishing to fall back into dreams with them, but most of the time you won't be able to.

And it won't make any sense, so later that day you'll fold an origami swan.

And you'll be reminded of them at the oddest times.

When you are about to wash your hair
in the shower, when you are on the
train staring out the window, when you
notice their favorite food on the menu
or at the market, when you wait in line
and glance down at your watch, when
you see a dandelion or a bumblebee,
when you somehow catch a whiff of
them on the air, when you finally get
the news you've been waiting for and
you pick up the phone to share it with
them ...

And it won't make any sense, so you'll put down the
phone and you'll fold an origami swan.

And you won't miss them as much as you think you should.

And some days you'll miss them more than you think you should. More than others say you have any right to miss them.

But **deep** down, in the place where you **know** things, like who you really are and what they truly meant to you, you'll **know** that doesn't make any sense, so you'll fold an origami swan.

And you'll miss the way they said hello.

And you'll miss saying hello back.
The sound you made when you'd call out to them.
The feeling of the sound of their name in your mouth.
You'll wonder why you didn't talk more.

And you'll wonder how many times, in total,
your lips opened and closed around their name,
around the special name you used just for them,
but you won't even be able to begin counting.

You'll forget the number that comes after seven.
And you'll forget to eat breakfast. You'll forget to
close the door. Forget to say thank you. Forget to
let the dog out. Forget to comb your hair. Forget
                                    what comes next.

And it won't make any sense.

So you'll do some of the things you forgot to do, clean up the mess and attempt to fold your lunch napkin into an origami swan. It will not work.

And some days it will hurt so bad, **the missing**. And you'll feel hollow and empty, but you'll notice it doesn't feel like nothingness. Not exactly. More like how an echo isn't a voice. More like vastness, openness. And you won't want to feel open on these painful days. Instead, you'll want to coat everything in a thick, sticky darkness. And you'll slam every open door. And you'll raise your voice. And you'll let the pitch black overtake you. And you'll be gone for a while. And you won't know how to get back, but you will **always** come back. And you will somehow.

You will come back.
Eventually.

you will.

And it won't make any sense, so you'll fold an origami swan
and think of nothing at all.

And some days you will hate them.

And you'll be so mad, so angry. And
you'll scream and lose your temper about
something completely unrelated. And it
won't make any sense because you know
it's not true, but you'll still be mad, so
you'll fold an origami swan. And you'll
rip it up in your own hands or crumple it
up and toss it in the garbage bin. And
you might get it out again. And you
might not. And you might feel better.
And you might not.

And you'll miss yourself and how you were
when you were with them.

And you'll miss the part that they – almost as if through some sort of alchemical reaction – brought out in you.

And you'll wonder if it's still there.
And it is, but you'll still wonder.
And you'll long for those days you spent together,
and for those hours, minutes, moments
And you'll see them in your mind's eye
and it'll play like a film clip on an endless loop.

And it won't make any sense,
so you'll fold an origami swan and
watch the loop play again and again

and again.

And you'll worry that you didn't do what you should've done. And you'll worry that you might've done more or done things differently. And you'll worry that you failed them in a way. That you could've done more. That you should've done more. And that they realized all this and felt disappointed in you, **but they didn't and they weren't.**

Time flows in only one direction.

And the hours won't make any sense,
so you'll fold an origami swan and
in time you'll forgive yourself.

And you'll have folded a lot of swans by now.
And you'll look up what a group of swans is called.

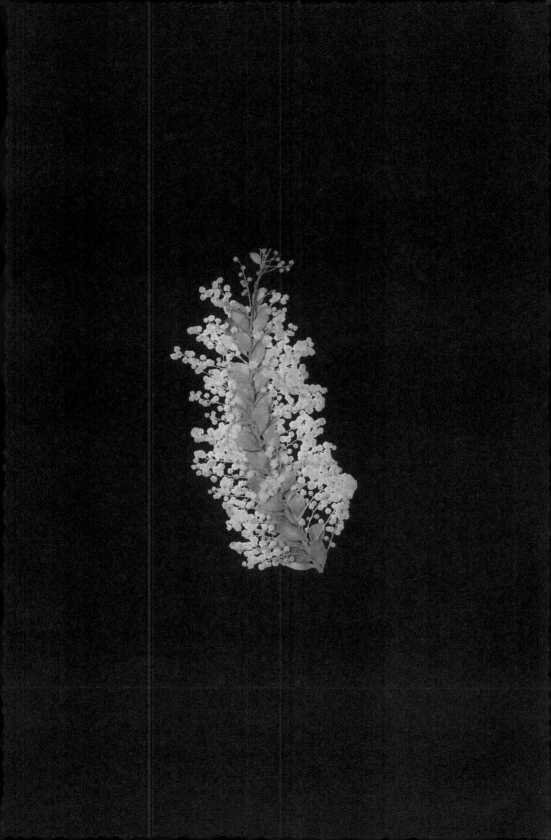

A ballet.
A group of swans is called a ballet.

And then you'll think how they would've loved to know that. And how you would've loved to tell them. And you'll think how perfect it is: **a ballet of swans.** How ballerinas float across the floor. You'll think of those pink satin slippers and how dancers must be in so much pain at times, but how they move seemingly without effort. And how they must have worked so hard to get that way. **That effortlessness is strength.** A swan above water, majestic, and under the surface, kicking like mad.

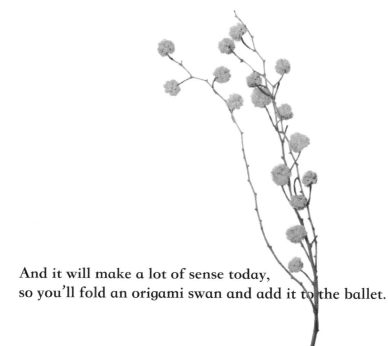

And it will make a lot of sense today,
so you'll fold an origami swan and add it to the ballet.

Sometimes you'll feel happy.
And it will feel strange,
even wrong.

And you'll think that if you were truly sad, you wouldn't be able to smile. And you'll feel guilty. And you'll be mistaken. It's okay to smile.

We feel many things at once.

And you'll laugh at how silly it all is. And you'll laugh as the tears stream down, and you'll fold an origami swan.

And you'll cry.
Some days will be about crying
and today might be one of those days.

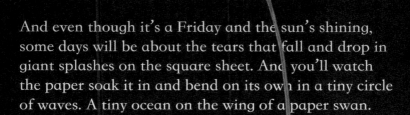

And even though it's a Friday and the sun's shining, some days will be about the tears that fall and drop in giant splashes on the square sheet. And you'll watch the paper soak it in and bend on its own in a tiny circle of waves. A tiny ocean on the wing of a paper swan.

And it won't make any sense, so you'll fold a soggy origami swan.

And you'll think about how once you fold a sheet of paper, you can never truly unfold it. How you can open it back up, but the creases will still be there.

And you'll think about how every moment with them was like them folding you into a paper you. And even if you took yourself into your own hands and, one by one, unfolded each corner until you were a giant sheet, the creases would still be there. And it wouldn't matter how long you waited, when you looked again, you'd still see them there. The creases, like the memories, don't ever leave us.

Not truly.

And it makes a lot of sense,
and you'll fold an origami swan
and you'll press the edges down hard under your fingernail.

And time will pass.

As it does.

And Time will pass.

Sometimes it will pass too quickly.

And you'll see a swan on a postage stamp, or you'll see an advertisement for Swan Lake, or you'll see a swan on the water and you'll think of them. You'll see the V in the water that trails in their wake, and you'll think of them. You'll see a V-formation of geese in the sky and think of them.

You'll see a bird, a feather, a quill, an old letter,
and you'll think of them.

And you'll think of them.

And you'll never stop thinking of them.

And it will make all the sense in the world
and you'll fold an origami swan
and you'll think of them.

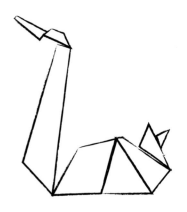

skipping ahead to the silver

lining of every dark

cloud isn't your practice

To all who helped bring this book into the world, in every small and grand way, **thank you.**

Thank you.

Dear reader,

First, let me commend you: caring for things outside of ourselves is a brave endeavor. After all, love is the thing that makes the suffering worth it. Now, please don't let me lead you astray – skipping ahead to the silver lining of every dark cloud isn't your practice. Loss isn't something you get over, like crossing a bridge. Instead, like a bird watcher with binoculars, season after season, observing is your practice. Through observation, you will come to know your grief intimately, yet, you will have little control over it.

Yes, watching is your practice. As much as you can, simply observe your emotions as they come and go. Notice how your understanding develops and the aspects that were once curious, evolve simply into the traits of the migrating fowl you have come to watch day after day. Breathe. Laugh when you can. Cry when you need to. And think of them.

Yours in grief and origami,

Saint-Michel

This book was created with the Japanese design aesthetics of Ma and wabi-sabi in mind.

As we experience loss of all kinds, these aesthetic approaches may be beneficial to consider.

I miss him
I want to hold him again and
kiss his little nose; I want to hug him
and hear him saying 'more' pointing to
a chocolate and then see him ~~little~~ making his funny
face, I want to dress him, bathe him
teach him how to ride a bike; I miss
you so much my son, mummy is
always with you, you are forever in
my heart, I will never forget the joy
and love you brought to our lives
the days pass, but the pain seems to
intensify, your sister keeps us going
and the crazy things we've been
through on the past month are beyond
~~kaha~~ cruel. We will get you to your
place of rest, so we can get some
peace too knowing you are layed amongst
the trees.

Michèle Saint-Michel—born in northwestern Missouri, the daughter of a farmer's daughter and a railroad-man's son—was raised by a salesman and a librarian. She found herself shelved between the art books and fantasy. She spent much of her childhood barefoot, baking mud pies and traipsing through the woods. She wrote and danced and talked quite a lot before she moved to the mountains. After some time in the snow and ancient shorelines, she grew tired of the landscape, so she set off to see more of the w   o   r   l   d   .

Saint-Michel fell madly in love with the sea and an oceanographer. She wrote this book after surviving a difficult time in her life, including the passing of her father. The book was illustrated by Saint-Michel from a log cabin, a stone's throw from the swift and muddy Missouri river. These days, she lives her life mostly unshelved, making experimental films, creating art books, writing letters, and pressing flowers. She hopes to one day grow a small poetry forest and set eyes—once again—on the sea.

This is the first book of her work to be published.

Also, from Michèle Saint-Michel, look for
"Draft Letters to a Certain Oceanographer" and
"Saint Agatha Mother Redeemer"

MICHÈLE SAINT-MICHEL